Anonymous

Dinner Commemorative of Charles Sumner

and Complimentary to Edward L. Pierce, Boston, December 29, 1894

Anonymous

Dinner Commemorative of Charles Sumner
and Complimentary to Edward L. Pierce, Boston, December 29, 1894

ISBN/EAN: 9783337092573

Printed in Europe, USA, Canada, Australia, Japan

Cover: Foto ©ninafisch / pixelio.de

More available books at **www.hansebooks.com**

DINNER

COMMEMORATIVE OF

CHARLES SUMNER

AND COMPLIMENTARY TO

EDWARD L. PIERCE

BOSTON, DECEMBER 29, 1894

CAMBRIDGE
JOHN WILSON AND SON
University Press
1895

Executive Committee.

WILLIAM CLAFLIN.

GEORGE F. HOAR.   FRANCIS V. BALCH.

ALANSON W. BEARD.   GEORGE A O. ERNST.

THE INVITATION.

Hon. EDWARD L. PIERCE.

DEAR SIR, — We desire to congratulate you on the accomplishment of your great work, the Life of Charles Sumner. It will always be among the highest and most trustworthy authorities in regard to the history of the great transactions in which Mr. Sumner took part, especially the overthrow of slavery and the foundation of the Republican party. Three things were essential to the successful performance of this task, — loving sympathy with the great character it was your duty to portray, absolute fidelity to truth, and literary capacity of a high order. All these you have possessed and manifested in amplest measure. Your name will always be inseparably associated with the great events you have narrated, and with the character you have portrayed.

Will you do us the honor to meet us and others of your friends at dinner, at a time and place to be hereafter fixed, that we may express to you in person our satisfaction with your work, and that we may revive the noble and stirring memories of Charles Sumner's career, and of the great political contest with slavery?

BOSTON, Dec. 1, 1894.

NAMES

OF THE

SIGNERS OF THE INVITATION TO MR. PIERCE, AND OF THE PURCHASERS OF TICKETS TO THE DINNER. THOSE WHOSE NAMES ARE MARKED WITH AN ASTERISK (*) WERE PRESENT.

*Adams, Charles Francis
*Aldrich, P. Emory
*Allen, Frank D.
*Allen, Nathaniel T.
*Allen, Walter
Allison, William B.
*Baker, John I.
*Balch, Francis V.
*Beard, Alanson W.
Bennett, Edmund H.
Bigelow, John
*Bird, Charles Sumner
*Bishop, Robert R.
*Blackwell, Henry B.
*Blanchard, S. Stillman
*Blunt, William E.
*Bolles, Matthew
*Borden, Simeon
*Brayton, John S.
*Bumpus, Everett C.
*Burr, Isaac T.
*Capen, Elmer H.
Candler, John W.
*Carter, Josiah H.
*Cate, George W.
Chadwick, John W.
*Chamberlain, Mellen
Chandler, William E.
*Churchill, J. P. S.

*Claflin, Adams D.
*Claflin, Arthur B.
*Claflin, William
*Codman, Charles R.
*Crapo, William W.
*Crocker, George G.
*Davis, Edward L.
*Davis, Robert T.
Dawes, Henry L.
*Doherty, William W.
Douglass, Frederick
*Endicott, Charles
*Endicott, William, Jr.
*Ernst, George A. O.
Fisher, Milton M.
Forbes, John M.
Fox, Charles B.
*Fox, William H.
*French, Asa
Fuller, Robert O.
*Gaffield, Thomas
*Goodell, Abner C.
*Goulding, F. P.
Green, Samuel A.
*Greenhalge, Frederic T.
Hale, Edward Everett
Harris, Benjamin W.
*Haskell, Edward H.
Hawley, Joseph R.

*Heywood, Frank E.
Heywood, Samuel R.
Higginson, T. Wentworth
*Hill, Hamilton A.
Hoar, E. Rockwood
*Hoar, George F.
*Hoar, Rockwood
*Hoar, Samuel
*Hollingsworth, A. L.
*Hopkins, W. S. B.
Houghton, Henry O.
*Hunnewell, James F.
*James, George Abbot
*Jenks, Henry F.
*Johnson, Arnold B.
*Johnson, Samuel
*Lane, Jonathan A.
Lodge, Henry Cabot
*Marsh, Henry A.
*McClellan, Arthur D.
*McPhail, A. M.
*McPherson, E. M.
Monroe, George H.
Morrill, Justin S.
*Morse, Elijah A.
*Morse, Robert M.
*Newhall, Lucian
Phillips, Stephen H.
*Phillips, Willard P.
*Pickard, Samuel T.
*Pierce, Charles Sumner
*Pierce, George B.
*Pillsbury, Albert E.
Platt, Orville H.
*Pratt, Laban
Purvis, Charles B.
*Rice, Alexander H.

*Rice, William W.
Robbins, Royal
Robbins, Royal E.
*Roberts, Louis A.
Ropes, John C.
*Salisbury, Stephen
Shattuck, George O.
*Sherman, Edgar J.
Sherman, John
*Stackpole, J. Lewis
*Stearns, R. H.
Stebbins, Solomon B.
*Stevens, A. W.
*Stoddard, Elijah B.
*Stone, Eben F.
*Stone, Henry
*Storey, Moorfield
Swift, John L.
*Taft, Royal C.
*Talbot, Newton
*Thayer, Charles M.
Thayer, James B.
*Wales, Nathaniel
Walker, Francis A.
*Walker, George
*Walker, Joseph
*Walker, Joseph H.
*Ware, Horace E.
*Washburn, Henry S.
Washburn, John D.
Weeden, William B.
White, S. V.
*Winslow, John
*Winslow, Samuel E.
*Wolcott, Roger
*Woods, Henry
*Wrightington, S. C.

MR. PIERCE'S REPLY.

MILTON, Dec. 10, 1894.

GENTLEMEN, — I acknowledge gratefully your appreciative estimate of my accomplished task and the invitation which accompanies it. It will give me great pleasure to meet friends who have joined in such kindly testimony, and to revive on the occasion, as you have suggested, the memories of Charles Sumner's career and of the historic struggle which his name will always recall.

I am yours very truly,

EDWARD L. PIERCE.

To Hon. WILLIAM CLAFLIN,
   Hon. GEORGE F. HOAR,
   Hon. CHARLES FRANCIS ADAMS,
      AND OTHERS.

PROCEEDINGS AT THE DINNER.

SATURDAY, the 29th day of December, 1894, was selected as the day for the dinner, which was given at the Parker House, Boston. After an informal reception to Mr. PIERCE, the company sat down to dine shortly after two o'clock. At the end of the hall opposite the Chairman was a bust of CHARLES SUMNER, draped with American flags. At each table was a souvenir menu card bearing a portrait of the guest.

A blessing was asked by Rev. ELMER H. CAPEN.

At four, Ex-Governor WILLIAM CLAFLIN called the company to order, and said, —

No man in public life more fully represents the principles which guided Charles Sumner in the great work which he did, — principles which are dear to the people of Massachusetts, — than our senior Senator. I am delegated by the Committee of Arrangements to invite him to preside on this occasion, and I now present him to you.

Senator GEORGE F. HOAR was welcomed by three rounds of applause, all the guests rising.

SENATOR HOAR'S ADDRESS.

Governor Claflin and Gentlemen, — On this occasion and at this gathering of the few survivors and the many representatives of the men who performed a great work for human freedom on this continent more than forty years ago, I can only say for myself, with Saint Paul, that I am the very least of the apostles, and am not worthy to be called an apostle. We have come together to recall something of the touching and noble story of the men who found slavery intrenched in this country in every department of the government, dictating law for the legislature, action for the executive, decisions for the bench; when to have any opinion in opposition to it meant banishment from every opportunity of public distinction and from most opportunities of private business; who gathered themselves together, a little company, and continued the battle until no slave was found anywhere under the American flag.

Before the year 1848 there had been a few men, never to be mentioned but with honor, who supposed the method of overcoming this great evil was to go out and to shake the dust off their feet against the Constitution and the country itself, and to renounce the American citizenship which was stained with that crime.

There were a few others, known as the Liberty Party, who practised upon a principle which we hear of occasionally now, of voting for the best men without regard to party, — who supposed that by here holding up the hands of a Democrat and there holding up the hands of a Whig, and there holding up the hands of nobody, they might accomplish something.

But in 1848 there were a few men — in Massachusetts chiefly, but in some other States also — who concluded that the way to govern a country on sound, clean, wise, political principles was to have a sound, wise, and clean political party with which to govern it.

I have made no preparation for this occasion except to draw off from memory a list of names of the men who were the leaders and the accomplishers of that work. I may possibly have forgotten one or two, — I have looked at no book or record, — but here is the list with which my memory supplies me : —

CHARLES FRANCIS ADAMS, who recalls a name famous for two generations in the annals of liberty, uttering a sentence which was his by hereditary right: " Sink or swim, live or die, survive or perish, I give my hand and my heart to this cause."

RICHARD H. DANA, the peerless master of English speech, who gave himself in his high social position to the cause of the poor and lowly fugitive slave.

JOHN G. PALFREY, who attacked slavery in that famous pamphlet of his with a vigor which Junius never attained and with a moral purpose of which Junius was incapable.

CHARLES ALLEN, perhaps in intellectual force the very foremost and greatest man of his generation, before whose simple authority Daniel Webster himself gave way.

SAMUEL HOAR, of whom it may not become me to speak; but still, in this assembly of his friends and the sons of his friends, I may say of him, after forty years have gone by, what Emerson said of him when he died, —

> " With beams December planets dart
> His cold eye truth and conduct scanned ;
> July was in his sunny heart,
> October in his liberal hand."

STEPHEN C. PHILLIPS, princeliest of Salem merchants.

WILLIAM CLAFLIN, who almost alone of that honored company is here to-day; the story of whose life is the story of every righteous and generous cause; whose friendship, with that of his accomplished and charming wife, has been the delight and the solace in their darkest hours of Sumner and Wilson and Whittier.

ERASTUS HOPKINS, the vigorous debater and leader in legislative halls, the last of the River Gods.

SAMUEL H. LYMAN, the accomplished gentleman and host, whose hospitality made even the beautiful valley of the Connecticut more beautiful and delightful.

CHARLES P. HUNTINGTON, the judge, the advocate, the stainless gentleman.

CHARLES SUMNER, leader of all these leaders, king of all these kings.

HENRY WILSON, Vice-President of the United States, the example and the promise to every poor boy, and to the father and mother of every poor boy, of what an American citizen may attain with the love of excellence and the love of freedom in his heart.

ANSON BURLINGAME, the silver-tongued orator whose voice summoned the youth of Massachusetts to duty like the sound of a trumpet.

WILLIAM S. ROBINSON, the wit, the scholar.

JAMES T. ROBINSON, who withdrew himself to a judicial station too early for his own fame and for the interest of the State.

ADIN THAYER, the greatest organizer of righteousness in Massachusetts since Sam Adams.

AMASA WALKER, the distinguished writer on political economy, now so worthily represented by the foremost of American economists, his son, Gen. Francis A. Walker.

ROBERT T. DAVIS, who is with us to-day; to whose

speech when a young man, in the Fall River town-meeting, the instruction was owing which decided the great contest when Mr. Sumner was elected Senator in 1851.

JOHN G. WHITTIER, RALPH WALDO EMERSON, HENRY W. LONGFELLOW, WILLIAM CULLEN BRYANT, JAMES RUSSELL LOWELL, GEORGE WILLIAM CURTIS, — need any American youth doubt that Liberty knows how to take care of her children, when you remember the career of the men whose names I have read?

JOHN P. HALE, candidate of the Free Soil party for the Presidency in 1852.

JOHN A. ANDREW, whose speech rang out over the hills and valleys of Massachusetts glowing and stimulant as a sermon of Paul.

SAMUEL G. HOWE, knightly champion of Freedom on two continents, who gave eyes to the blind, to the deaf and dumb articulate speech, and brought light and cheerfulness to the darkened cell of the insane.

FRANK W. BIRD, affectionate, generous, and most independent of gentlemen.

HORACE MANN and HENRY L. DAWES, who came into our ranks a little later, but whose titles to the undying regard of the people of Massachusetts are too familiar to need repetition.

Every one of these men whom I have named was able single-handed and alone to have led in this movement, and to have encountered and to have overthrown any antagonist the American continent could have brought against him. We have come together to honor their memories. They are gone, with one or two living exceptions. The love of fellow-citizens, the pride of honored ancestry, the memory of brilliant service, the matchless youthful vigor as you and I, sir, remember them to-day, have not saved them from the inexorable doom.

> "Stemmata longa patrum, magnaeque potentia famae,
> Quicquid forma potest addere, quicquid opes,
> Expectant pariter non evitabile tempus."

To-day is given to the memory of CHARLES SUMNER. I will not undertake to add anything to the emotion which the memory of that simple name must excite in the bosom of every gentleman who sits by this board. Our friend, whom we have asked to be our guest to-night, has given the best years of his life, all the accomplishments of his early education, every power of his intellect which might have brought him success and fame in any of the walks which the Republic opens to him, to embalm the memory of Charles Sumner for the admiration of posterity. The great work has been well done. I do not think of anything that is wanting in this matchless biography. A loving sympathy with his subject, judicial impartiality, fairness to antagonists, untiring industry, — all these he has possessed in an uncommon degree, I may almost say in a degree unexampled in the annals of biographical literature. Mr. Pierce's name will go down in history, and will abide, by the side of the great name of the man whom he has commemorated, so long as the memory of this contest for liberty abides in the hearts of the American people.

I have received a good many letters from gentlemen, far and near, who sympathize with the object of this meeting. I will not read them now; you will have an opportunity of seeing them hereafter. I will make one exception; that is the exception of Mr. GEORGE W. JULIAN, one of the earliest and ablest leaders of the movement for the political overthrow of slavery, and candidate of the Free Soil party for the office of Vice-President in 1852.

IRVINGTON, IND., Dec. 26, 1894.

GENTLEMEN, — I have your favor of the 17th, inviting me to attend a dinner in Boston, on the 29th, commemorative of Charles Sumner and complimentary to Edward L. Pierce. I regret most sincerely that advancing years and failing health will make this impossible. It would indeed be one of the delights of my old age to join the surviving friends and admirers of Mr. Sumner in honoring his memory, and in thanking his biographer for the great work he has accomplished. I waited long for its completion; but I waited patiently, because I felt assured that the perfect consummation of his task would justify the delay. It called for great labor, tireless diligence, perfect devotion to the truth, genuine sympathy with his subject, the gift of judicial fairness in dealing with the relations of Mr. Sumner to other public men, and rare literary skill. All these requirements have been happily met, and we thus have a complete portraiture of Charles Sumner in all the varying phases of his grand life. Indeed, it was a great honor and a priceless privilege to write such a biography; and Mr. Pierce, in building this magnificent monument to his friend, has linked his own name imperishably with that of Sumner, whose rank in the army of reform and among the heroes of humanity will be second to that of no other American.

I am yours very truly,

GEORGE W. JULIAN.

Hon. GEORGE F. HOAR,
Hon. WILLIAM CLAFLIN,
  AND OTHERS.

SENATOR HOAR: Mr. Sumner, in his grand national career, never forgot his love to the State that bore him, and gave him the only commission for public service which he ever held. It is fitting that, at this meeting to honor his memory, the first voice heard should be that of the Commonwealth he so dearly loved. I ask you, my friends, to listen to his Excellency, Governor GREENHALGE.

THE GOVERNOR'S ADDRESS.

MR. CHAIRMAN, FELLOW-CITIZENS, — I am aware that I stand in the presence of the Commonwealth,— in the presence of its intellect, of its conscience, of its highest sentiment. I have, therefore, responded to the request that the official voice of the Commonwealth should be heard.

You meet here on a most impressive occasion, — to celebrate the completion of a work which commemorates the white flower of a blameless life spent in the cause of liberty, and of those ideas which seem always to have found a fertile soil in the Commonwealth of Massachusetts.

When our great Senator read the list of those who had been collaborators with Sumner in the mighty work which he performed, while there was a feeling of elation there was something also of depression, until, looking over this assembly, it seemed to me that the list of the guests here to-day would furnish some eloquent man, fifty years from now, with a list not entirely unworthy of comparison with that read by our senior Senator.

What a remarkable gathering this is, my friends! I stand before you with a feeling of diffidence and trepidation. It is, I recognize, a memorable occasion. I can only add my feeble word of tribute to the great soul whom you commemorate here to-day; and I have had no opportunity to meditate on what I say. I wonder what the Senator would have done had he prepared an address upon this occasion, if the matchless words which have fallen from his lips are the result of the lack of preparation! Yet even now there is echoing in our ears the mighty eulogy, worthy of its mighty subject, of Daniel Webster, the Atlas who supported and sustained alone the burden of the Constitution and the Union against all enemies. Webster belonged to that earlier epoch. The work of men is as distinct as the epoch in which they live.

And then we come to this next epoch, when his great work — and I do not want that to be minimized because the light of a later day had not come to him — was taken up by the powerful hand of Sumner, and to the Union and to the Constitution was given the ineffaceable glory of liberty and equality.

My friends, this is a worthy tribute not only to that illustrious name, deathless in the list of the great names of the country; it is a proper and well-merited tribute to the faithful, impartial, and truthful biographer here present with us, — and it is a noticeable fact that the biographer was a part, as it were, of the events which he himself describes. The Chairman has well eulogized the great work which praises the workman. We know of so many broken columns in literary effort that I think we may all congratulate our friend and guest upon the fact that he can write "Finis" after his great work, as really completed. When we think of Macaulay, who only began a history; when we think of Buckle, who never got beyond an introduction; when we think of the many fragments which have come down to us as histories, — we may congratulate you, sir [*turning to* Mr. PIERCE], that you have been permitted to finish this elaborate and graceful work.

I am here only to say, my friends, in the name of the Commonwealth, that, if I may be permitted, the Commonwealth on this occasion shall be converted into a hall of statues; and in that hall the figure of Sumner must always occupy a commanding position, requiring the reverence and the gratitude of every child of Massachusetts, of every man who loves the truth and the inspiration of freedom.

I thank you, Mr. Chairman and Gentlemen, for the privilege of being a part of this occasion.

SENATOR HOAR: Charles Sumner had many friends who loved him and whom he loved. If he were to choose among them all the name he would like to have linked with his own twenty years after his death, there would have been no one he would have preferred to that of the guest of the evening. I ask you, my friends, to rise and drink to the memory of Charles Sumner, and to the great work of his friend and biographer.

The company rose and joined in drinking the toast, after which the Senator added : —

I have now the pleasure to present to you Mr. EDWARD L. PIERCE.

After the cheers which greeted Mr. PIERCE as he rose, he spoke as follows : —

MR. PIERCE'S ADDRESS.

MR. HOAR, GOVERNOR CLAFLIN, AND FRIENDS:

IT has sometimes occurred to me, when taking part in a festivity where honor was being paid to a particular guest, that he must sit uneasily while others spoke his praises. I have, however, to confess that such an experience, which is to-day my own, has proved thus far rather a pleasure than a pain. But, grateful as I am for the pleasant words which are being said of myself and my toils, I cannot fail to recognize that the presence of this company here is not so much a friendly testimonial to myself, as a tribute (using Milton's words) to the memory of "a brave man and worthy patriot, dear to God and famous to all ages." If such commemorations are more frequent in this community than elsewhere, they call for no apology. We do not envy sister States that outrun our Commonwealth in numbers and resources, for we count always as her most precious possession the character, the public service, and the renown of her sons.

It will be fifty years the next Fourth of July that I first saw Charles Sumner. It was in Tremont Temple, when he delivered his oration on the "True Grandeur of Nations,"—an oration which first made him known to the world. I was a boy of sixteen from the country, and was passing the holiday in the city, mostly on the Common, where, like others of my age, I indulged in cake and lemonade, and exploded firecrackers, spending in this mode of celebrating the day the one or two ninepences which had been allowed me for pocket-money. Always interested from boyhood in public speaking, I sought the Temple, having heard casually that an address was to be given there. I recall still the scene,—the orator wearing a blue dress-coat with gilt buttons, white waistcoat and trousers; on his right and left officers of the army and navy in uniform, and behind him a choir of one hundred school-girls clad in white. I heard his opening sentences; but the allurements of the Common proving stronger with me than his voice, I soon left the hall. Later, I returned in time to hear his tender tribute to Sir Philip Sidney, which perhaps I might now repeat with something of his tone and gesture. The vista of the orator's future did not open before him at that hour; and least of all did he foresee that near the entrance of the hall, in perhaps his youngest, certainly his obscurest, listener, was one who was thereafter to tell to mankind the story of his career. Three years later, in 1848,— a year which in the Old World as in this was to many a new birth of thought and aspiration,— I heard Sumner in Faneuil Hall, as he took the chair at a meeting called to ratify the Free Soil nominations of Van Buren and Adams, and joined in the applause as he finished, then giving my first open adhesion to the movement. By this time I had become an enthusiast for him, and let pass no opportunity of being present at his addresses. I may say here that it is difficult at this day to realize the power and inspiration that he was with the young men of that period. This came from the charm of his personal presence, the glow of his rhetoric, the mellow cadences of his far-reaching voice, his unmistakable sincerity, his courage, and his moral fervor: it was these which then swayed ingenuous youth. The next year, when I was in college, forty-five years ago this month, I confessed in a letter to him my admiration of his character, accompanying it with some things I had published, and received promptly in return an invitation to call on him. I remember freshly that first meeting, in his back office, in No. 4 Court Street, the site of the present Sears building. To me it was a great moment; and my feelings as I entered were perhaps not unlike those of a lover on the point of making his declaration. His gracious welcome at once put me at ease. Indeed, he had always time for young men, — time to talk with them, time to write to them, time to encourage in them every prompting to intellectual and moral endeavor.

That was the beginning of a friendship which lasted to the end, without the slightest break or misunderstanding. I delight to remember that it was a relation in which there was no thought of mutual gain or advantage. He never assisted me to an office, rarely ever gave me an introduction, and, so far as I know, I have never had a dollar which came to me, directly or indirectly, through him; and yet I can truly say, that there was no moment in that relation of twenty-five years when I would not have made any sacrifice and encountered any peril in his behalf. It is for others to say whether fidelity on my part has been prolonged beyond his life. Nor will I believe that this devotion to him was exceptional with myself. Sumner, as I have had occasion to say elsewhere, stands alone, or almost alone, as a public man whose support was in the moral enthusiasm of the people. He had this rare advantage, — that at every critical point of his career he could rally to his side a host of men to whom he had never done a favor by help to office or otherwise, and who expected no such favor in return. What a bulwark such a force is to any public man! How far superior to any army of retainers and hustlers!

It is proper, in this connection, to say that in this intercourse between a distinguished public man and one much younger than himself there was no self-assertion on the one side or unmanly deference on the other. I was always frank in questioning to his face his position or his action, as frank as I could be with any of yourselves. Once or twice, when I was quite a young man, others put on me the duty of saying to him things which they did not like to say themselves. He never took offence, but always kindly received such criticisms. So much for my personal relations with him of whom I have written.

Sumner in his will designated Henry W. Longfellow, Francis V. Balch, and myself as his literary executors, with full power to preserve or destroy his papers; but he made no suggestion then or at any other time as to the choice of a biographer. That was a matter which did not seem to concern him; but his interest centred in his last years on the preparation of a complete edition of his speeches, which he sometimes spoke of as his " Life." The executors, myself as one of them, invited several distinguished writers to undertake the service; and after they had declined, the duty, by request of my associates, fell to myself. I began at once to collect materials, at the same time laying aside my studies for a law-book on which I was then engaged. It was fortunate that the work was entered upon at once, as otherwise much that was valuable would have perished. Since then have passed away his mates of the Boston Latin School, the members of his college class save one,[1] the one sister who survived him, his early friend and law-partner, Hillard, most of his associates in the Senate (only Sherman, Morrill, and one other still remaining there), and nearly all who were intimate with him in the earlier political conflicts in which he took part.

The first two volumes, which only brought Sumner to July 4, 1845, the day when his public career began, were published in 1877. It seemed proper to fill so much space with this early period, as it covered his foreign journey in the years 1838–1840, and his association with the European jurists and scholars of that time. The last two volumes were not published till 1893, just nineteen years after his death. The task was on my mind for the entire period, though for three or four years after the publication of the first two volumes I mostly suspended the work in order to finish my law-book. For about fifteen years I devoted my time chiefly to the memoir, except during such vacations and excursions to Europe as seemed necessary for health and relaxation. It is difficult to comprehend the labor in such research before composition begins, — forty thousand letters to Sumner from correspondents to be examined, and notes made from them; thousands of his own letters collected from every quarter, and selections to be made; files of newspapers for thirty years to be turned over, with more or less to be copied; histories, biographies, public documents, the congressional debates for a quarter of a century, to be studied; a large corres-

[1] Dr. Jonathan F. Bemis, the last surviving member of the class of 1830 in Harvard College, died eight days after this reference to him.

pondence to be conducted, and interviews to be sought
with all contemporaries who could illustrate or freshen a
narrative with their recollections. Sometimes I journeyed
to places associated with interesting episodes of his life, —
to Aix in Savoy and Montpellier in France, in both of
which resorts he lingered, waiting for the health and vigor
which for nearly four years so often retreated as he thought
himself about to grasp them. Nor in this search did I
omit a visit to the grave of Preston S. Brooks in Edgefield,
S. C., being the first, if not the only, Northern man to
stand before the memorial stone of one who impersonated
the madness and desperation of a losing cause. Some may
think this manifold toil superfluous; but it seems to me
that biography and history are of little worth when the
writer shrinks from such drudgery.

The manuscript of the last two volumes as prepared for
the printer filled twenty-six hundred pages. All was twice
written, and some parts three or four times. Every page,
indeed every sentence, was carefully weighed, and original
sources again and again explored for verification. The
whole was read by the late George William Curtis, who
advised the reduction of one chapter; but otherwise this
kindly critic made only slight suggestions. It was a grief
to me that this dear friend of my own did not live to greet
the publication of the volumes in which he had taken so
earnest and prolonged interest. I may add that I have no
faith in fine writing, or in the inspirations of genius, at
least in historical composition; but I believe profoundly
in exhaustive research and painstaking fidelity to truth.
These commonplace virtues tell in the long run.

Sometimes journalists and my own friends have chided
me for a too long interval between the first two and the
last two volumes; and one or more have reminded me
that a final biographical sketch of myself was likely to be

called for before the completion of Sumner's memoir. While I was the recipient of this friendly pressure, I was all the while working to the limit of vital forces, which, happily, have been stronger with me than with most men.

Necessarily with every biographer his own subject will occupy the most conspicuous place in his canvas; but it is his duty to do justice to other characters of the same period, whether fellow-combatants or antagonists. This I endeavored to do, — sometimes assigning to one or another of Sumner's contemporaries the prime leadership in a contest in which he also bore an eminent part. It was a satisfaction to reveal, perhaps more clearly than before, the noble qualities of his colleague, Henry Wilson; and to bring to the front the genuine patriotism and masterly ability of Salmon P. Chase, who, as one of the only two Free Soilers then in the Senate, welcomed as a coadjutor a champion of freedom from Massachusetts.

There is one duty of a biographer which I regard as supreme. It is to reveal fully his subject to mankind; to suppress nothing; to avoid no part of his career which has been exposed to criticism. Two of Sumner's devoted friends, both scholars and poets, advised me to pass lightly over two of his controversies, — one with Winthrop in 1846 and 1847, concerning the Mexican war; and the other with President Grant's Administration. After reflection, it seemed to me that it was neither the part of courage nor of wisdom to maintain silence as to those well-known events; and that it was the duty of the historian to tell not only the truth, but the whole truth. I confess that I had many troubled thoughts about the controversy with Winthrop, anxious as I was to adhere faithfully to historical verity, and at the same time not to wound the sensibilities of an aged man whose high personal character entitled him to sincere respect. It was a relief to be assured soon after the final volumes appeared, that, while he might dissent on some points from my view of those questions, he considered himself courteously and fairly treated.

The suggestion has been made that Sumner's biography is of too ample dimensions; that life is too short to allow readers, even those not overburdened with public or private cares, the time to traverse so much ground. I was quite well aware that this objection might be raised, but on reflection felt bound to disregard it. The four volumes comprehend letters as well as narrative; and they are not more voluminous than the memoirs and correspondence, published separately or together, of other public men, Americans or Europeans, who have had a long and remarkable connection with public affairs. Besides, a complete biography is always a thesaurus which can be drawn upon by the authors of briefer lives, more suited to the tastes and wants of readers who cannot spare the time for a full investigation. I recall with pleasure an encouraging message sent to me by Senator Hoar some time after the first half of the work appeared, bidding me to take all the space I required to carry out my original design, not withholding a word which the spirit moved me to write.

A critic for a New York city journal, probably wearied with the multitude of books laid on his table, and having no time to traverse the period covered by my volumes, undertook, instead of reviewing, to count, or rather estimate, the total number of words in the entire biography. This was a novel mode of treating historical composition; and seeking myself a standard of comparison, I set an amanuensis to computing the words in a Sunday newspaper of thirty-six or forty pages. The result was instructive as well as surprising. My four volumes were equalled

in the number of words by two and one half copies of such a hebdomidal issue. I asked my critic to consider whether the product of fifteen years of labor might not be of as much use to posterity as two and one half numbers of a Sunday newspaper.

The full study of Sumner's public life reveals what is new to many, — the variety of the subjects which commanded his attention, comprehending not only the Antislavery cause, of which he was the protagonist in Congress, but also foreign relations and nearly all domestic interests which came up for consideration in his time. On financial measures he was among the soundest of the sound ; and on these and other questions, some of which combined a moral as well as a material side, he escaped the vagaries and extravagances which have too often disfigured the careers of agitators and reformers.

No public man, or none except John Bright, has stood as Sumner did for the supremacy of the moral sentiments in government and the intercourse of nations. That is to be his distinctive place in history. Lord Brougham has singled out as a test of the progress of our race in wisdom and virtue its veneration in successive ages for the name of Washington. In like manner, will not a measure of our country's loyalty to the law of right and duty be found in all time to come in its fidelity to the precepts and example of the statesman we are now commemorating?

While honor is justly paid to the senator who for nearly a quarter of a century represented Massachusetts, to me the thought has ever been present that like honor belongs to the generation of her people who recognized at the outset the nobility of his character, and stood by him faithfully to the end, never failing him at any hour, and supporting him always in his advanced positions. In the reaction of

1862, when a combination was made for forcing him from public life, he was rewarded with a complete vindication. When at an earlier period he was compelled by his disability to forego public duties for nearly four years, there was no murmur calling for a surrender of his seat. If one Legislature, misinterpreting public opinion, passed on him a censure, its successor hastened to expunge it. Fortunate the statesman who has such a people behind him! It is doubtful if a career like his, unbroken and triumphant to the end, could have been had elsewhere than in this Commonwealth.

It is a rare assembly before whom it is my privilege to stand this day. Here are citizens of honorable repute of our own and other States, some of whom have borne the insignia of high office, and are to live in the history of the country. I see here and there those to whom I have been bound for long years by bonds of friendship and community of thought. I recognize also the faces of old comrades who enlisted with me in youth in the cause of freedom, and who, after a hard-fought contest ending in blood, rejoice at last in a redeemed land, where there is no master and no slave. Here, too, are veterans whose service in its ranks had an earlier beginning than my own. I need hardly express to you, to each and all, my profound appreciation of the generous thought implied in your presence on this occasion. You come here not to exult over the issue of any party contest; you come to testify your admiration of a great character, who, you are pleased to believe, has been well placed before his countrymen and posterity. I am devoutly grateful to God for having permitted me to see the end of my appointed task; and while life remains to me, I shall cherish the memory of your sympathies and congratulations.

SENATOR HOAR: Among the most brilliant periods of the civic history of Boston, and among the most brilliant periods of the civic history of Massachusetts, must be counted the administration of the mayor and of the governor, Alexander H. Rice. But he has a more brilliant title still to be remembered in gatherings like this. Governor Rice, during a large part of the civil war, was the chairman of the Committee of Naval Affairs of the United States House of Representatives; and his rare business ability, his vigor and eloquence in debate, very largely contributed to the accomplishment of the legislation which resulted in bringing our navy to a height of excellence, in the closing years of the war, to which the navy of no other nation on earth ever before attained. Mr. Rice's name must always be mentioned with honor when the history of the war for the Union is adequately written. It is not necessary to say here that no meeting in Massachusetts where he is present ever dissolves with any degree of satisfaction to the men who compose it, unless they have heard from him. I ask you to listen to the Hon. Alexander H. Rice.

EX-GOVERNOR RICE'S ADDRESS.

IT is wholly owing to your gratuitous kindness, Mr. President, that in this assembly I am called to take precedence of the brilliant and eloquent gentlemen whom I see round this table. I should be very glad indeed if I could add anything of interest to what has been already said.

We are assembled here, as we all know, to pay our tribute of affectionate respect and gratitude to the memory of Charles Sumner. I came also, I am glad to confess, to pay my affectionate tribute of respect and friendship to his biographer. This is not one of my best days, and I might have excused myself from coming here; but when I thought of the man to be commemorated and the man to be complimented, I believe I should have come if I had known I should be taken home in a hearse!

So much has been said and so much is known of Mr. Sumner that it would be inexpedient for me to attempt, with my partial and imperfect knowledge of him, to add anything to what is contained in the volumes which have been written and in the speeches which have now been made. If I may indulge in a word of reminiscence, I would say that when I was a boy and first came to Boston, my habit was to pass my evenings wherever public speaking was to be heard. Among the earliest occasions to which my recollection goes back, was that in which Mr. Sumner had a discussion with some other leading Bostonians on the subject of prison discipline, and I went to hear him in the old Tremont Temple. I cannot say that I altogether espoused the views and sentiments expressed by Mr. Sumner on that subject. But the brilliancy of his discourse, the bewitching enthusiasm of his speech captivated me; and among the examples of clearness and force of expression I have ever attempted to follow, and to imitate as far as might be, have been those of Mr. Sumner.

It was not my privilege to be born early enough, or at least to get into affairs far enough, to catch the particular spirit and the particular doctrines which he early advocated and exemplified, and which gave him great celebrity. My sympathies at that time were with what may have been termed the conservatives, though so far as I had any political attachment it was to the Antislavery wing of the Whig party. Men in those days regarded Mr. Sumner as a radical. If he were living to-day, we should count him a conservative. At all events, we have come forward so far and so rapidly that we adopt his views without inquiring whether they are radical or conservative. They have become the platform of the great mass of the American people to-day.

It was my privilege to know Mr. Sumner in Washington during the critical period to which you, sir, have referred. He was always brilliant; he was always active; he was always prophetic; he was always fearless; according to my recollection he was not always so hopeful as some men were. He never believed that the country would perish any more than he believed liberty would perish; but he was impatient for the accomplishment of the great result to which he, in common with all patriotic Americans, was looking forward.

I remember that sometime after the war it was my good fortune to be chairman of the committee to erect a statue of Mr. Sumner, the one which now stands in the Public Garden. That statue will last as long as bronze can endure in the open air, but I do not think it will stand so long as the great monument which our friend, Mr. Pierce, has erected in literature to him. Whether the one or the other or both shall decay, the memory of Charles Sumner is certain to go down through the ages with imperishable renown.

At the time that the statue to which I have alluded was erected, or when it was projected, invitations were sent far and wide to sculptors, not only in America but in Europe, for models in competition. I think sixteen models were submitted from some of the most eminent sculptors in the world, men and women; and it was a very interesting matter to study the designs that were sent. Many of them were from artists who had never seen Mr. Sumner personally, but who knew him only by reputation; and it appeared as if each one had endeavored to submit his own, or her own, ideal of a great, noble-minded, able, and patriotic statesman. Well, sir, we had among those sixteen models a great variety; and they taught me this lesson, which I have had frequent occasion to apply ever since, — it has been of use to me in my judgment of public men and characters, — namely, that a man is what he is in himself, and what he knows himself to be, and what those who are very near him know him to be, rather than what he is represented to be by some hasty or incompetent critic to the miscellaneous public. Each of these sculptors, I concluded, embodied his own ideal of Mr. Sumner. He did not make Mr. Sumner as he was in reality, but presented his own ideal of what such a man as Mr. Sumner might be. Therefore the designs varied according to the capacity and genius and moral character of the artist; consequently, among the designs submitted were models which would convey to strangers characteristics varying all the way from John Bright, the illustrious statesman, down to a Pennsylvania beer-seller. And so it is with the criticisms that we sometimes get of public men, their characters and methods. These criticisms are not necessarily representative of the men themselves, but of the quality of the writer. I have in my possession now one of the best of those models of Mr. Sumner, and I cherish it at a higher and ever increasing value as time goes on. I may say, however, that it is a model which fitly represents my ideal of Mr. Sumner after an acquaintance of years, rather than my earlier and imperfect idea of him.

But I did not rise to talk of myself. I had no expectation of being called upon to say anything. But I wish to concur with you in saying that among the choicest heritages of Massachusetts are the lives of the great men who have adorned her history and ennobled her society. Among those I may safely say there stands no one superior to him whose memory we now commemorate. And when we look up, as you have done, to the galaxy of the great men of our State, I feel certain that there, in letters of imperishable light, will forever shine the name of Charles Sumner.

SENATOR HOAR: One of the leaders in the movement of which we have spoken set the example of freeing his own slaves and accepting for himself a life of what might almost be called poverty, rather than to take wealth by the inheritance of human beings. I allude to John G. Palfrey. His widow is now dwelling, at the age of nearly ninety-five, in his house at Cambridge, and I am sure it would gratify her and her children to receive the salutation of this company. I ask you to drink to the health of Mrs. Palfrey.

After the toast, Senator Hoar continued: —

I was present, a boy of twenty-two, at the meeting in Worcester, on the 28th of June, 1848, when the Free Soil Party was organized; and I remember well the scene when Charles Francis Adams rose and addressed that meeting with the sentence which I have quoted upon his lips. It seemed to me as if the portrait of old John Adams had come down out of the canvas, and as if all the associations of liberty and of American patriotism which for more than a hundred years had clustered round that name, were invoked to give strength and support to the cause. Mr. Adams had the rare good fortune to follow his father and his grandfather as the representative of this country at the Court of St. James. The three were there in the three most trying periods of our history. Indeed, I think that our diplomacy has been almost boy's play except that which this grandfather, father, and son conducted for us. The elders here can remember something of the infinite patience with which that man kept his fiery soul in peace until the opportune moment came, when it was his privilege to put in writing what seems to me the single most eloquent sentence in the political annals of America. When Lord John Russell wrote to him that her Majesty's ministers had come to the conclusion that they had no power to interfere with the going out of the rams from Laird's ship-yard, Mr. Adams replied, "It is superfluous to observe to your Lordship that this is war," and the rams were stopped. We have here this afternoon a gentleman who fitly represents that name and those traditions. And though I do not always agree with him,— and I do not believe there was ever an Adams who ever had anybody always to agree with him,— yet if we want a good example of sturdy Americanism, and of sturdy, old-fashioned American Puritan character, to send into the desolate regions of New York or elsewhere, I think I would on the whole be willing to trust Mr. Charles Francis Adams anywhere.

MR. ADAMS'S ADDRESS.

MR. CHAIRMAN,— I do not understand that we are here this evening either for the exchange of compliments, or to discuss the Adams family. You have just remarked that you did not believe there had any one ever lived who in all matters would have agreed with the various members of the Adams family. In passing, I will only ask in reply whether the same remark would be wholly pointless and altogether inapplicable, were the name of Hoar to be in the criticism substituted for that of Adams?

But, coming to the matter more properly in hand, I will say that this has been to me an extremely interesting occasion. In compliance with a suggestion to that effect, I had prepared quite a speech for it, but on the whole have concluded to cast what I had thus prepared aside, and, following the impulse of the moment, indulge in recollections; then, after I have in this way fired my volley, I propose to fall back, and give way to others who will better entertain you.

As I listened to Senator Hoar and Mr. Pierce and Governor Rice, my memory flew back, over a longer period than I care to specify, to the time when I first knew Charles Sumner. He was then the most intimate personal friend my father had, and his face and figure were familiar in the house. Two or three trifling incidents of those days bring him back to me very freshly; and as, though in no way important, they are not wholly inappropriate to the occasion, I propose to refer to them.

The first, I remember I repeated once before, it must have been nearly twenty-five years ago, at a dinner of "The Bird Club," as it was called, — and would that Frank Bird, as they who knew him called him, might have been spared long enough to be here with us to-night; but *Dis aliter visum*, the voice of the veteran is silent forever! — it was at a meeting of the Bird Club, I say, more than a score of years ago, under this very roof, — perhaps, indeed, in this very room. Mr. Sumner was the guest of the day, and as such made some reference to the events of earlier times as compared with those great scenes which the country had then recently passed through, for the Rebellion was suppressed, and slavery only recently abolished. I was a younger man then; but, as I remember, I was presently called upon to say something, and my mind again, as this evening, reverted to the past; so, turning to Mr.

Sumner, I asked if he remembered a little evening incident at my father's house, photographed on my memory. It must have occurred now more than forty years ago, before Mr. Sumner was a senator. It was at that period — those days of bitterness, thank Heaven, are gone forever by! — when John Greenleaf Whittier was writing the "Ichabod;" the period when Mr. Webster still dominated in the Commonwealth, and Sumner, my father, and those who agreed with them were a small and despised minority. We were sitting in the dining-room at the house in Mount Vernon Street, No 57, where my father then lived, and where, more than thirty years later, he died. I, a mere boy, was then at school, and that evening, as many other evenings, I listened, as I conned my Virgil for the next day's lesson, to the conversation, as it went discursively on. Suddenly, I remember, Mr. Sumner broke out with intensity of feeling, saying, "Yes! yes! — everything now is against us, but we will win in the end; the cause is sure to win; it cannot but win!" A line in Virgil just then caught my eye, and, looking up from my book, I repeated it to Mr. Sumner, suggesting that it might have a certain applicability to the hereafter. It was the familiar line, — I had never heard of it before, — *Forsan et hæc olim meminisse juvabit.* I remember further, Mr. Sumner looked at me, his face lighting with a smile, and asked, "Is n't that in the first book of the Æneid, about the 220th line?" He was a good classical scholar, and his memory had this time served him well; it was the 203d line; and, had I only glanced four lines further down on the page I should have come to this not less apt exhortation, —

Durate, et vosmet rebus servate secundis.

Yet another scene comes back to me, — a scene which, considering the subsequent lives and work of the parties to it, I have often thought of since with strong tendency to mirth. It was at the old house at Quincy. Mr. Sumner, the guest there for some Sunday, and taking a deep interest in my father's children, was most companionable in his peculiar way with all of us. It was before I was yet in college. He got talking with us, as he was wont to do, earnest for our improvement. My younger brother, Henry Adams, has since attained distinction as a writer in the field of history. He was there, and Mr. Sumner was endeavoring in his rather direct way to instil into him a love of historical study. My elder brother, John Quincy, was also there. Finally, I remember Mr. Sumner in his appeal used this expression, no less homely than strong, "Why, Henry, I am sure you never would let a slice of pudding stand in your way to a slice of history!" Suddenly, my brother John spoke up very greatly to the point, "You bet your life, Mr. Sumner, he would n't let it stand in the way *long*." I can see still the puzzled look of the Senator over the great enjoyment of the future historian at the realistic turn thus given to the exhortation.

One more incident, — an incident which brings upon the stage my friend Mr. Pierce, as well as other memorable characters. The scene shifts to England; and the time last summer only. I was in the cathedral of Peterborough, when I saw Mr. Pierce's name written in the visitor's book directly above my own. I went through the noble edifice until I found him, and we walked together up and down the grand Norman nave and transept. He spoke of his book and of Sumner, and then suddenly said, "By the way, a curious thing; I wonder if you can throw light upon it. When your grandfather died, in 1848, your father sent to Mr. Sumner 'a slight token,' as he described it, as a remembrance of your grandfather, not saying what it was. I found his note among Mr. Sumner's papers, but have never succeeded in getting any trace of the article. You wrote me some years ago that it was a silver ring, which, to correct the tremulousness of his hand, your grandfather wore to steady his pen in writing. Have you any idea what became of that ring after Sumner's death?" "Yes," I replied at once, "I can tell you exactly what became of it. In the first place it was not a ring at all. I was mistaken. I knew that my father at that time sent such a ring to Dr. Palfrey; and my strong impression was that he had sent a companion ring to Mr. Sumner. I so wrote to you. But since then Judge E. R. Hoar has incidentally told me that, when Sumner died, his sister sent to him (Judge Hoar) two silver sleeve-buttons which my grandfather was wearing at the time of his death in the Capitol at Washington, and which my father had then sent to her brother." That was the "slight token;" and was it not singular that our friend, Mr. Pierce, after seeking high and low for a solution of that little American biographical puzzle, dating back more than twenty years, should suddenly find it as he paced up and down in the dim light of the ancient cathedral of Peterborough!

A few days afterwards we both returned to America, and I shortly, being now a near neighbor of his, called on my old friend, Judge Hoar. He is not here to-night. Of all living men he should be here; but the end cometh, and the places which knew him will soon know him no more forever. But, as I was saying, soon after my return I called to see him at his home; nor shall I soon forget the look of genuine pleasure which lighted up that rugged, familiar face, and the exclamation, "Why! Charley boy!" which broke out, as he welcomed me back. Rarely have look and involuntary exclamation given me keener and more lasting pleasure, — from that source it was a compliment, than which none greater.

Then, as we sat on his porch, looking out on the quiet tree-shaded Concord road, and chatted in the pleasant October afternoon, I mentioned among other things the incident of the "little token" and Peterborough cathedral, and how singular it was that our friend here should at last have found trace of it when and as he did. Judge Hoar agreed; and then, referring to those sleeve-buttons, he suddenly turned and said, "Do you know, I've been thinking I ought to leave those to you!" I do not know or greatly care whether he really does it; but I do know how gratified I felt when he said it. That "little token" has a genealogy; it is a veritable *transmittendum*, — John Quincy Adams in 1848, Charles Sumner in 1874, Ebenezer Rockwood Hoar in 1895: it is a goodly parentage! If the "little token" should now, indeed, pass on to me, I shall be but a trustee. Who next?

But passing from anecdotes, and remembering that this occasion is devoted not only to Mr. Sumner, but to our guest, it may be said that the time has now come when we can fairly venture to strike a measure, not only of Mr. Sumner as a public character, but we can also in some degree estimate the place which Mr. Pierce's biography of him will occupy in historical literature. I am of those who believe in evolution and sequence; and it was the great good fortune of Mr. Sumner, as well as of Mr. Pierce, that the life of the first and the story of that life by the other are connected with one of the great epochs — the crises and turning points — of human history.

We have most of us lived long enough to know that in many respects history is what Macaulay in one of his copies of verses described it, — "but a nurse's tale;" none the less, from the time when man first struggled up from the ganglion through the ape into his present form and movement, there have ever been periods that marked a distinct advance in his progress, — sudden upward movements to a higher elevation than he had before attained. For myself I cannot survey the record, stretching back beyond the first dawn of recorded history, and understand the pessimist. It seems impossible even to suppose that the upward tending career of man has reached its culminating point in this year of grace 1894, or that it will do so for yet centuries to come. But one thing in it is very noticeable: while the tendency as a whole has been upward, the movement has ever been not steady and slow, but uneven, — by leaps, long pauses, and sudden bounds. It is a trite old saying that happy is the country and the age which have no history. True! but it offers a poor field for the biographer. Our friend and guest of the evening was more fortunate. The record over which he labored was the record of one of those great forward bounds to which I have referred, which mark epochs; and in it the man, the story of whose life he had to tell, was prominent among the foremost.

In the history of our country there have been exactly two of these epochal periods. Those two were the war of Independence, and the years of Constitutional reconstruction which followed it; and, later on, in our own days, the agitation which preceded and followed the clash of arms of 1861. Mr. Hoar has just said the war of the Rebellion had for its outcome that there was no master and no slave left throughout our land. In thus putting it, he must permit me to say, I think he belittled the subject. The result far transcended our territorial limits, no matter how considerable those limits may be; for, like the shot of the embattled farmers of 1775, that April clash of arms was heard throughout the world. Just as in the last century our war of Independence struck the key-note and served as a prelude to the French Revolution and the catastrophic

European upheaval which followed, so the emancipation of the slave in the United States through the clash of 1861 led to his almost immediate emancipation throughout the civilized world. It was no contained or local movement. Nor, though this was much, was it all. During four centuries now, ever since Columbus made his land-fall on the shores of the Western Hemisphere, two great issues have constantly presented themselves before civilized, advancing nations, and over them the battle has raged. Those issues, constituting the theme of modern history, were religious freedom and the equality of man before the law. Our war of Independence established in the last century the principle of equality before the law, so far forth as the Caucasian was concerned; our war of the Rebellion established it for the human race. Thus it was epochal. In it and through it the race made in its process of evolution a forward bound.

It was a great, a memorable drama; and it remains for the biographer and the historian to assign his proper part to each of the actors in it. But as yet we lack a proper perspective, — we are not far enough removed from the men and the events to see them in correct proportions, and in their true relations with each other and with the other men and other events which preceded and came after. Even to attempt this now, we — still men, though no longer young men — who took part in that great drama and knew personally its now historic characters, — even to attempt this, I say, we must project ourselves into the future; and, so projecting ourselves, imagine, if we can, where and how those men and events will stand two centuries hence, when they become to our descendants in the seventh generation what the great English rebellion, with Charles Stuart, Cromwell and Strafford, Hampden, Pym, "Canterbury" and Clarendon for the actors in it, is to us.

Thus projecting ourselves forward in the slowly revolving cycles, let us this evening look back from the new standpoint in the now far removed future, and, forecasting the verdict of posterity, try to class Charles Sumner, and assign to him the place he will hold in the final summary. He will then have been weighed in the balance.

Of statesmen, so-called, there are many varieties. And first there is the great influencer of events, the all-round statesman, so to speak; the man who, correctly appreciating the trend of events, divines, either through instinct or reflection, the result towards which the aspirations of his contemporaries and the forces in operation are working, and, himself in harmony with them, has the supreme faculty of biding his time, knowing when to be quiescent and when to strike : and so, patiently welding together with master hand elements once discordant, at last the hour strikes, and he is in position and has the power to bring the desired result about. And he does it! Thereafter the conditions of the world are different from what they were before. These are statesmen of the first class ; and of these our century has, in my opinion, produced but two, — Bismarck and Cavour : men who have unified peoples and called nationalities into being.

That Charles Sumner was of this class, no one who knew him would for an instant contend. His was not the eye for the entire field, nor his the calm judgment and iron, self-controlling will ; too fervid and intense, he could not bide his time, — he could not hold his peace. He was a statesman of a wholly different stamp from these.

There is then the statesman who with well-ordered mind and even temper looks with observing eye at the social and material influences at work, at the new forces science is placing at the disposal of man. He listens to the student and philosopher, is recipient of new ideas. Again, he also, calmly watching the turmoil around, knows instinctively how long to be silent and when to speak. The interpreter of the prophets, he is the model administrator among practical men. He establishes some national policy along the lines of which nations will continue to develop when his statue has for generations stood in the market-place. Such was Robert Peel.

Then there is the statesman of yet another class, the man who, having a natural faculty for supremacy and command, instinctively personifies a people or a class, — feels as they feel, sees as they see, acts as they want to act, and says what they wish to hear in the way they like to hear it. A statesman of this sort is born, he does not make himself; and he influences and controls less through his individuality than from the fact that he typifies others, — in him they see themselves. Such a statesman was Palmerston; he typified the average Englishman, — in him they saw themselves.

Charles Sumner was of the class of Peel, or of the class of Palmerston, no more than of that of Bismarck or Cavour. He was not an administrator. In moments of emergency he could not control himself or his utterances; and he who cannot at all times control himself and his own tongue can never control those about him. Not knowing when to strike, he can never be depended on to strike at the right moment. Those about do not gather to him and lean up against him in the hour of crisis, instinctively looking for guidance and support. Charles Sumner had none of this. Sumner, on the contrary, was an idealist, a *doctrinaire.* He saw a great principle, — he saw it clearly, and he grasped it; the principle, the idea, also grasped him, — possessed him wholly. He could not place himself in the position of his opponents, observing them and justly weighing their motives: indeed, he could not see things from another and different point of view from his own. He represented an idea; and on behalf of that idea he vehemently appealed to his fellow-men, — and his fellow-men responded. His hold on them was moral. He was thus, in his field and day, the statesman *doctrinaire*, and as such a great and necessary dynamic force; and so he played his part.

When, therefore, as I see it, two hundred years hence, — in the early years of the 22d century, — the philosophic historian shall these events narrate, nothing extenuating nor aught in malice setting down, he will speak of Sumner as the Henry Vane or Edmund Burke of our Rebellion period. And when he does so, he will turn to the volumes of our friend at the head of the table, and they will have the lasting value which belongs to the statements of one who was himself part of the events of which he wrote. His work is not a mere detailed study of the past. Far otherwise: the events he described he himself participated in. It will then be for the future historian, as it would be for us if some Hyde had two hundred and fifty years ago, in his stately and sonorous prose, recorded at the moment the words and acts of Vane, or some more studious and dignified though not less patient and devoted Boswell had told us, as an eye-witness, of the pure career and lofty motives of Burke.

SENATOR HOAR: We must be pardoned if those of us who are Massachusetts men may seem to have dealt a little too exclusively with Massachusetts memories. But let us not forget that gallant band who even against heavier odds held up the torch of liberty in the metropolis of the country, in New York. We have one of them here to-night, —

a gentleman whose name has recently been synonomous with good and honest work for the public good there, and who brings to us the recollections of the Antislavery days, and who bears a name that has been fragrant and honored in Massachusetts since the Pilgrims landed from the "Mayflower." I ask you to hear Mr. John Winslow, of Brooklyn, New York.

MR. WINSLOW'S ADDRESS.

Mr. Chairman and Gentlemen, — This is indeed a most interesting occasion, and I am here from New York because I am in deep sympathy with the purpose of this gathering. I have been thinking a little of the early training which our distinguished guest had, and which was the beginning of that kind of equipment which made him the success he is as the biographer of Charles Sumner. As this occasion is largely in honor of Mr. Pierce, as associated with the life and times of Sumner, some personal reminiscences may be interesting. I suppose there is nobody present who has known our guest any better or longer than I have. In his early college days, the tidings I had of him was that he was a prize-winner, — not as an athlete, not as a rower of boats, or foot-ball player, but as an excellent writer in English composition. Then, a little later on, when he and I were together in the Cambridge Law School, I remember with what abounding energy he entered upon his work. I thought I had some of that quality, but I could never go around as he did; he was a worker. Five or six of us became rather marked men at the Law School because we had the courage to assert our Antislavery views. There were about fifty students at the Law School from the South who were not at all backward, but very aggressive, in telling us in our debates, in our so-called parliament and elsewhere, the poor opinion they had of all Antislavery folk. In our last term the faculty gave us for a prize dissertation, "The consideration of a contract at law and in equity." Those Southern young men were ambitious, and most of them contended for the prize. I confess the satisfaction some of us had when it was announced that Mr. Pierce, one of the few out-spoken Antislavery men, was the winner. I have spoken of the energy of our friend. If it had not been for this inborn trait we should never have had the benefit of these four volumes. Now, that was the kind of life in those early days that was equipping our friend for the splendid work he did in these fifteen years of which he has spoken. He never seemed to tire in studies and researches. It was said that in one summer vacation, when most students were resting, he read "Story on Promissory Notes," and found it a satisfactory recreation.

The impression that Charles Sumner has left upon the people of this country is so profound that it seems superfluous to add many words as to his distinguished career. The oration on the "True Grandeur of Nations" came out in 1845, and brought its author into prominent notice. It was a masterly exposure of the evils of war. I read it, and wondered how a man could be so learned and so industrious, make so many historical and other apt citations, and have such brilliant thoughts. It is true I was a little puzzled, not to say a little "rattled," at the peace propositions of the oration. I was in the habit of thinking that defensive fighting, at least, was all right. I used to think that if an Indian tomahawk came uncomfortably near the scalp of a Pilgrim Father, he would be justified in protecting his protecting scalp. When the Revolutionary War broke out, it seemed all right to fight it out: hence Lexington and Bunker Hill. And more than ever when the war for the

Union came, I thought that it was profoundly right to fight our enemies who were uprooting our institutions; and I have no doubt that Mr. Sumner came to the same view. I never heard that he voted against appropriations to support the Union army. It is interesting to notice how the main propositions of that famous oration were received by leading men of the times. A clergyman, a friend of Mr. Sumner, then a theological student at Andover, wrote that he was obliged to dissent. Judge Story wrote, complimenting him for the great ability displayed and the learning shown, but that he must dissent. I remember Horace Mann and Dr. Lieber and others wrote to the same effect. Jeremiah Mason, a personal friend of Sumner, and the peer and contemporary of Daniel Webster at the bar, told him " an anti-war society is as little practicable as an anti-thunder-and-lightning society." Wendell Phillips wrote in his characteristic way that he had not read one word of the oration, but was sure it was all right, good, and true because he noticed that some of the Boston papers were attacking it. A few weeks later Phillips wrote again, saying he had read it, and "'T is a good thing, nobly done, and will make your name dear to many whom you will never hear of. I went with you in almost everything, here and there margining a *de hoc quaere*." Many others expressed approval. While few of us could agree with the position taken as to war, yet we see in the argument of the orator a noble aspiration for the things that make for peace, and that may promote a higher and better life among the nations.

What makes this occasion specially interesting is that in some degree our life has entered in upon the life of Sumner. There are men here who remember hearing the oration to which I have alluded. There are men here who glowed with pride and happiness when it was announced in 1851, after a memorable struggle, that he had been elected United States senator. There are men here who were cast down in deep gloom and sorrow when they heard that Brooks had struck his cruel blows upon the defenceless head of the Senator in the Senate chamber. So our lives, those of us who are elderly men, may be looked upon as identified in various degrees with the life and the toil and the sufferings and triumphs of Charles Sumner.

It seems to me that by some eternal law men are raised up to meet the crisis at hand. So it has been in all the ages. When the American Revolution came, Washington was the leader needed. What man had we in this country better fitted for the great Antislavery debate than this fearless and able man, Sumner? In that debate, whether in the Senate or before the people, he excelled in moral feeling and courage and ability. In debating the aggressions and outrages of the slave-power Sumner appeared conspicuously in the Senate, resolutely denying that slavery was an institution; he declared it was a barbarism. When the war for the Union came, there appeared at last, though it seemed as though the right general never would appear, Grant, Sherman, and Sheridan. In the trying times of the Civil War Abraham Lincoln was the man needed as President. And so it has ever been.

This memorial of Sumner is appreciated not only in this but in other countries. The " Westminster Review " said of it : "Mr. Pierce's familiarity with the lives and careers of former celebrities in Parliament, on the bench, or at the bar, is another illustration of how much there is in common between the peoples of the United States and of England, how the fame of our statesmen and advocates is amongst the cherished possessions of America." I might make other quotations from the press of other countries, showing that this memorial work has more than a local reputation. Not all of us may know how much of learning, of wonderful industry, honest and often obscure toil is given to such a work. Thackeray said of the works of his friend Macaulay: "He reads twenty books to write a sentence; he travels a hundred miles to make a line of description." A similar remark is applicable to almost any considerable historical work written with ability and fidelity; such, for instance, as Parkman's twelve volumes, and others that might be named. These four volumes will stand as high authority as to our political history for the period they cover. It will not require a prophetic voice to trace in the bright outlines of the future the continued recognition of the noble career of Charles Sumner as exemplified in these books; and the delightful association of our friend with the great name, as biographer, will ever be remembered by his kindred and by his countrymen with appreciation and satisfaction.

SENATOR HOAR: We have a friend here who is keeping the torch of good learning aloft, a gentleman who lives "on the heights." We shall be glad to hear from Dr. Elmer H. Capen, the President of Tufts College.

DR. CAPEN'S ADDRESS.

MR. CHAIRMAN,— It is certainly a distinguished honor and privilege to be asked to speak in such a presence and on such an occasion as this, though I must confess the call is wholly unexpected. I came into the room almost at the end of the procession, and sat down very humbly, and ate my dinner in peace, greatly enjoying the conversation of my neighbors. The dinner was nearly over before I was informed, much to my surprise, that you had placed my name in the list of victims. But I suppose in obedience to your summons I must give an account of my presence here, and I assure you I do it very cheerfully. A number of motives have combined to draw me into this company to-day. First and foremost of all let me say, that I have come prompted by my long friendship and high regard for the gentleman to whom this meeting is a most just and worthy compliment. I have known him from my very early boyhood. I am indebted to him for favors rendered in my young manhood. He and I were born in the same town, and I come, therefore, as a loyal son of old Stoughton to rejoice in one of the fairest and noblest products of that ancient town, to join with you in the acclaim which is due to his achievements, to bask in the sunlight of his fame, and to appropriate some of the reflected glory of his life.

Let me also say that I was drawn hither by the magic name of Charles Sumner. That is one of the charms that I can never resist. The personality of Sumner fired my youthful enthusiasm as no other human being ever did; it called forth all the admiration of my mature manhood; and to this hour it is as potent as ever to rouse and quicken. I have sometimes thought that if I were wakened in the middle of the night and summoned to speak on his life and services, I should not falter or fail. But somehow this occasion seems to take away my power of utterance. This company of distinguished men, the renowned and graceful orators who have preceded me, have rendered me nearly speechless.

The hour is late, sir, and I will not take time for more than a single word. That word must bear directly upon the significance of this banquet. Why are we here? What is the spell that holds us? I have asked myself again and again while sitting at this board, what it is in the character of Sumner that brings together, twenty years after his death, such an assemblage of his admirers and followers? Is there another civilian in our American history, Abraham Lincoln alone excepted, who could call forth such a tribute to his worth and fame? Could even the great Webster himself? We have been reminded recently of the merits and achievements of that mighty champion of the Union and expounder of the Constitution. I have read, Mr. Chairman, — every gentleman in this room has read with a thrill of admiration, — your eloquent eulogy in the Senate of the United States upon the career of the majestic and peerless statesman who for so many years stood before the civilized world as the representative and type of all that is highest and noblest in this American republic. For myself I observed with delight the fine analysis of the speech, the accurate description and careful weighing of the wonderful powers of that wonderful man; above all, the portrayal of the grounds on which for more than a generation he was held almost as an idol in Massachusetts. It was a satisfaction to me also to note how, with unflinching courage and perfect fidelity to truth, you showed why, after all that idolatry, the hearts of the people fell away from him as if he had done some sacrilegious and evil thing, and left him to oblivion, ignominy, and death.

It seems to me, however, that your speech had a deeper meaning than appears to the casual reader. It ought to be said here that in that speech in which you have sketched so profoundly alike the triumph and failure of Daniel Webster, you have assigned the real reason why in the same hour that he was rejected Massachusetts turned, as if under the influence of a mighty loadstone, to the imperial personality of Charles Sumner; why it followed his leadership, not only in life, but follows it in death, and will follow it so long as the life-blood courses in the veins of her people. No public man was ever more ardently loved or more completely trusted. Both the love and trust were evoked by the moral grandeur of his life. The people followed his standard because he believed in holding governments to the eternal and unchangeable law of right; because he was true to the moral principles on which our beloved Commonwealth is founded; because he had lofty ideals, and never wavered in his devotion to them; because he walked reverently and loyally in the steps of the Pilgrims and Puritans, who, in the fear of God and the love of man, set up here in this western wilderness a nation whose foundation stones are human equality, universal freedom, and inviolable justice.

This, moreover, is the quality in the characters and offices of men in public life that abides. Other qualities shift and fluctuate, but this remains the same. Other qualities may dazzle and even dominate for a season, but this never loses its potency, but even grows stronger as time goes on. In conversation not long ago with Dr. Edward Everett Hale, he told me of an address which he gave at Brown University, in which, of set purpose, he drew the picture of two men. One was of the man who, when he was a member of the national House of Representatives from Rhode Island, and rose in his place to speak, emptied the Senate chamber; and who, when he was a senator from Rhode Island, and rose in his place to speak, emptied the House. The other was the picture of the great man who put the impress of his life on Brown University. He told me that when he had finished and stepped down from the platform, men born in Rhode Island, who were the contemporaries of the man described, came to him and asked him whom he meant by the man, who, when he was a representative and rose to speak in the House, emptied the Senate, and when he was a senator and rose to speak, emptied the House, — so completely had the memory and tradition of Tristam Burges faded from men's minds. The brilliant genius, the biting sarcasm, the eloquent speech had not sufficed to preserve him from oblivion. But there was no doubt about the other man. Whoever walks the streets of Providence to-day, whoever shall walk them for two generations to come, will recognize Francis Wayland as a living and abiding presence. It is so everywhere. Brilliancy of intellect, even commanding genius, cannot keep men alive. It is moral power alone that abides. Our ancestors sleep under the sod; the men who came in that bitter winter and made the settlement at Plymouth that they might "keep their names and nation" and "give their children such an education as they themselves had received;" the men who followed in their steps and settled here in Boston and the adjoining territory; the men who struggled and wrought for good government and pure morals in the Colony and Province of Massachusetts; the great men, represented in their descendants at this table to-day, who put the quality and stamp of their peerless characters into the constitution and civil order of this Commonwealth, and whose names are an inspiration to youth and a guide to the people, and will be to the end of time, — are all of them dead and in their graves. Yet they are still alive, and never were they so potent in their activity as now. They walk abroad; they speak with the living voice; we see them as we could not see them if they were still in the flesh, and they make to us and to all men an irresistible appeal.

Some men we know were impatient with what they called the extreme views and action of Charles Sumner. Not long before he died I spent a few weeks in Washington. While sitting in the gallery of the Senate I saw that whenever he rose to urge his Civil Rights Bill, senators in their impatience would spring from their seats, wheel round and rush into the cloak-rooms, leaving him to make his speech almost alone to the President of the Senate. He seemed to be regarded with something akin to hatred. At least, men could not conceal their indignation ; some even treated him with contempt when he tried to address them from the high moral plane of his convictions concerning freedom and equality. In a short time he died, with the words " Take care of my Civil Rights Bill " trembling on his lips. Then what a change took place! Around his open grave men forgot their animosities; every bitter epithet was recalled; the tumult of controversy was hushed ; strife and hatred vanished away ; the tenderest and most beautiful tributes to his memory were from those who had been his life-long enemies. And the Civil Rights Bill, what of that? The formal thing which bore that name dropped into "innocuous desuetude." But the " living creature " that animated it, the spirit that called it forth, was taken up instantly into the conscience and heart alike of America and of the whole civilized world. To-day it is no longer a question whether the negro shall have civil rights. Civil rights are accorded to all men, without distinction of race or color, by virtue of their manhood.

It is a great thing, a rare privilege, to have been the contemporaries and followers of such a man. A far greater privilege it must have been for our friend to have walked by his side, enjoyed his friendship, shared his counsels, received his confidence, won his affection, gathered up and put together the materials which will make both for the great Senator himself and his biographer an imperishable memorial. I congratulate Mr. Pierce on his noble achievement. I rejoice for the memory of Sumner that the mighty part which he performed in the most important epoch of the Republic has had so just and faithful and loving a chronicler.

SENATOR HOAR: There is one gentleman here whose presence seems like a message from the death-bed of Charles Sumner, — a gentleman whom Sumner loved, and who was with him during the closing hours of his life and when he died. We shall be very glad to hear from Mr. Arnold B. Johnson.

MR. JOHNSON'S ADDRESS.

MR. CHAIRMAN, — I shall not take your time in thanking you for the honor of calling on me to speak on this subject, or of the embarrassment of speaking all unprepared in this presence.

Mr. Sumner called me, a raw Cape Cod boy just from a fresh-water college, to his service, for no reason that I know except it be that I was a grandnephew of Tristam Burges, to whom the last speaker so eloquently referred, and that I was born in the same house in which Tristam Burges was born.

I was with Mr. Sumner from the early fifties through all his service in the Senate. I was with him before and after the assault of Brooks upon him, and during all his long illness which followed that dastardly attack. I was with him when he was deprived of the chairmanship of his committee. I was with him when he was again struck down by the hands of his mother, his own State; and I was with him when word came that the State had again taken him to her bosom. I was with him in the hour and article of death, and I followed him to Mount Auburn. And in all those years, and in all those trials, there was never a moment when he lost my respect, or when I bated one jot or one tittle of the love which he inspired in my heart.

Mr. Sumner did me the high honor to call me his private

secretary. It was a misnomer. It was impossible for him to have a secretary. I wrote his letters, and looked up specified authorities, and made fair copies. He did everything of importance with his own hand, and everything was marked by his own mind.

It has been said that no man can be a hero to his valet. It is certainly true that no man can be a hero to his private secretary unless, truly, he is a hero. I have been accused of hero worship, and I do not deny the accusation in this case.

I knew Mr. Pierce when I first went to Mr. Sumner. Mr. Pierce was then doing for Senator Chase what I was to do for the Massachusetts Senator. Mr. Pierce was my senior in age, as well as in experience; hence I took him for my model and for my standard, and what success I had was largely due to his example as well as to his precept. He soon left Washington, but our friendship thus begun has never been discontinued. During the time he was engaged on his great book we were often in correspondence, and I know by personal experience something of the trouble and pains he took, and the trouble and pains he remorselessly inflicted on every one from whom he hoped to get information with which he could fix a date or settle a fact.

As to the admirable book Mr. Pierce has produced, I know it well. There is nothing in it, big as it is, — and it could not be too big for its subject, — which does not belong there; and small as it is, compared with the work it chronicles, I cannot remember that anything which ought to be there is omitted.

The Mussulman's creed is, There is but one God, and Mahomet is his prophet. Let me by paraphrase give utterance to the feeling in my heart: There was but one Sumner, and Pierce is his biographer.

TRIBUTE TO JUDGE HOAR.

MR. PIERCE: I have a resolution to offer at this time, and for evident reasons I shall call for the vote myself, asking you to rise in voting upon it.

The following resolution was then read, and unanimously adopted by a rising vote: —

At a meeting of citizens of Massachusetts and other States held in Boston, Dec. 29, 1894, to commemorate Charles Sumner and to recognize the completion of his biography, the following resolution was passed unanimously and by a rising vote: —

We miss greatly, to-day, the presence of Hon. Ebenezer Rockwood Hoar, former Justice of the Supreme Court of Massachusetts, Representative in Congress, and Attorney-General of the United States, now confined to his home in Concord by illness. He was, as early as 1845, a coadjutor of Sumner in resistance to the extension of slavery, and their co-operation and friendship lasted during their common lives. It was a retort of Judge Hoar, then known as "a Conscience Whig," in the Senate of the State, which fastened the name of "Cotton Whigs" on those who were hostile to that movement. He hoped and endeavored at that time, though unavailingly, to make Mr. Webster its leader. He drew the call in May, 1848 (being now the last survivor among the signers), joining with Sumner, Wilson, Adams, S. C. Phillips, F. W. Bird, and others for the State Convention which founded the Free Soil party in this State. He drew the resolutions of the people of Concord at the time of the assault upon the Senator. He was at the latter's bedside during his last illness, held his hand in the supreme moment when life departed, announced his death in the House of Representatives, and shortly after delivered in that body a tender and eloquent eulogy on his coadjutor and friend.

Massachusetts has had no worthier among her cherished names than that of E. Rockwood Hoar, jurist, publicist, and faithful servant of freedom. It is to his and Sumner's credit alike that each was bound to the other in a lifelong friendship.

SENATOR HOAR: The resolution which you have adopted will give its comfort to one of the kindest and most loving hearts that ever beat. I do not know that any of you will ever see his face again in life. I saw him yesterday, on his sick-bed, and he spoke with great interest of this occasion, and charged me to give his love to all of those who were present, and I take pleasure in giving the message.

There is not a person present whose voice we would not like to hear. But the hours of the day, and of the week, are closing. I pronounce this meeting at an end.

Judge Hoar took great interest in the report of the dinner, which was read to him. His death followed a few weeks later, on Jan. 31, 1895.

LETTERS.

LETTERS.

LETTER FROM SENATOR LODGE.

WASHINGTON, D. C., Dec. 20, 1894.

MY DEAR MR. ERNST, — It will not be possible for me, I am sorry to say, to be in Boston on the 29th of December, and I shall therefore be unable to be present at the dinner to Mr. Pierce, which I very greatly regret.

Mr. Sumner was the friend of my grandfather and of my father and mother. He was constantly at our house down to the time of his death, and my earliest memories are associated with him in the days when he was suffering most and doing most for the cause of human freedom. It is a great gratification to me, therefore, both on public and personal grounds, that Mr. Pierce has brought to a conclusion a biography in every way so worthy of its subject. It is a real disappointment that I cannot be present to join with Mr. Pierce's other friends in extending to him our congratulations on the completion of his work, and our high appreciation of its value and merit.

Very truly yours,

HENRY CABOT LODGE.

GEORGE A. O. ERNST, ESQ.

LETTER FROM CARL SCHURZ,
Late Secretary of the Interior.

> Pocantico Hills, Westchester County, N. Y.,
> Dec. 25, 1894.

My dear Sir, — Accept my sincere thanks for your very kind letter which I received this morning. I regret exceedingly to find myself deprived by some engagements, which do not permit a journey to Boston on the 29th, of the privilege of joining you in doing honor to our friend, Mr. Edward L. Pierce, for the eminent service he has rendered the country by setting a worthy literary monument to one of the great characters in the history of this republic. Nobody can appreciate the extraordinary value of Mr. Pierce's work more than I do, having personally witnessed many of the important events it relates, and having known the persons active in them.

My inability to be present at your banquet I feel as an especially sore privation when I think of the relations of warm friendship which bound me to Charles Sumner, as well as of those which have for many years existed, and will, I trust, last as long as we live, between Mr. Pierce and myself. Believe me, dear sir,

Very sincerely yours,

Carl Schurz.

The Honorable William Claflin.

LETTER FROM EX-SENATOR DAWES.

PITTSFIELD, MASS., Dec. 28, 1894.

My Dear Mr. Ernst, — I had most certainly intended to be present at the dinner to Mr. Pierce to-morrow, and had hoped that nothing would prevent; but I am very sorry to find, at the last moment, that I cannot be there. I regret sincerely that I am not able thus to show my personal regard for Mr. Pierce, and my appreciation of the fidelity and exhaustive labor with which he has put upon the permanent pages of history the debt of the nation for the great public services and sacrifices of Mr. Sumner. I beg you to assure Mr. Pierce that considerations I cannot disregard prevent my being there. I am,

Very truly yours,

H. L. DAWES.

GEORGE A. O. ERNST, ESQ.

LETTER FROM CHAUNCEY L. KNAPP,

MEMBER OF CONGRESS, 1855–1859, NOW NEARLY EIGHTY-SIX YEARS OF AGE.

LOWELL, Dec. 29, 1894.

The stormy day keeps me at home, yet, with Hon. Edward L. Pierce's fourth volume on my table, I must not fail, though at long range, to congratulate him and the friends of freedom on the faithful discharge of a great trust, — at once a just tribute to an ideal statesman, whose great office was unsought, whose life-work shines over the world like a morning star.

CHAUNCEY L. KNAPP.

To Hon. WILLIAM CLAFLIN,
AND OTHERS, *Committee.*

LETTER FROM FREDERICK DOUGLASS.

CEDAR HILL: ANACOSTEN, D. C.,
Dec. 26, 1894.

DEAR SIR, — I very much regret my inability to be present at the dinner on the 29th of December, in Boston, given in honor of Mr. Pierce. You need no assurance from me of entire sympathy with that demonstration. No man to my knowledge has better deserved such a mark of esteem by his fellow-citizens. He has rendered to the country and the world a very large service in giving to the generations to come one of the very best histories ever written of the life and works of a public man. Mr. Pierce has done his work not less truly because he has done it lovingly. As to Mr. Sumner, the subject of it, no man who has known me at any time during these last fifty years has any need to be told of how highly I esteemed him or how grateful I have felt towards him during all these years. The name of Charles Sumner has seldom been absent from my lips or pen upon any fitting occasion. As I look back to the times when Mr. Sumner became a prominent actor as a statesman in national affairs, and view the condition of the two then existing political parties, and the choice then made of the side he took in politics, I am filled with admiration of the man. Conservatism at that time possessed large powers of temptation. The tide of reform was rising around it, and it naturally needed the support of a man of great learning, of splendid figure, and of brilliant talents, such as were possessed by Charles Sumner. He was an orator and a statesman, and the side he took in view of the times marked him as a moral hero. He stood on the mountain top where he could plainly see all that could minister to a worldly ambition, and the conservatism of Massachusetts at that time would have denied him nothing. Boston was proud of him, Harvard admired him, Massachusetts loved him; but neither the pride, the admiration, nor the love that was cherished toward him could swerve him from his chosen work in the world. To a mind other than his a certain degree of hesitation about taking the side he did might seem quite pardonable. The unpopularity of the cause he espoused, the hardships and dangers met with by any who thought, spoke, and voted on the side of the slave, caused even brave men to hesitate; but this was not so with Charles Sumner. He fairly flung himself into the thickest of the fight against the insolent slave-power, and with the fullest knowledge of the consequences involved in his act. He had seen the violence with which it had assailed John Quincy Adams, Joshua R. Giddings, and John P. Hale, and knew full well that the fury that assailed them would pursue him; but he met the facts with the calmness of conscious truth and right, and was prepared for whatever might come to him. No man ever stepped into the Senate of the United States with more courtly manners or noble bearing. His princely appearance and well-known convictions invited to him the combined assaults of the enemy. The slave-power saw in him at once a dangerous force. His whole manner and bearing told them at once that he was not a man to be trifled with. No man could play fast and loose with him. To accept him one must accept his principles, for he and his principles were one. No wonder that Preston Brooks resorted to the bludgeon; assassination was slavery's best weapon. No Judas Iscariot was needed to point out this champion of freedom. The assassin knew him at sight, and dealt his blow accordingly. Oh, what a day of agony was that which brought news to the oppressed that their champion had been struck down on the floor of the Senate! The blow was only surpassed by the assassination of Abraham Lincoln. Fortunately for us, though struck down, our champion did not die. He lived to see more of his mind, heart, and great purposes woven into the organic law of the land than has been the good fortune of any other statesman of our time. In conclusion, allow me to thank Mr. Pierce, on my own behalf and that of the millions I in some measure represent, for handing down to posterity a faithful, loving, and voluminous history of this truly great and good man.

FREDERICK DOUGLASS.

To Hon. GEORGE F. HOAR.

LETTER FROM REV. EDWARD EVERETT HALE.

ROXBURY, Dec. 23, 1894.

MY DEAR SIR, — I wish I might be considered among the hosts at the dinner given in honor of Mr. Pierce.

My own memory runs back far enough for me to recall much of the ground over which he has gone so well; and we have all been so much indebted to him through his useful life that I am glad that, while he is in the body, he may know how much we value him. Perhaps people of our blood are too apt to let their friends die without any idea of the estimation in which they are held.

Truly yours,
EDWARD E. HALE.

To Mr. GEORGE A. O. ERNST.

LETTER FROM JOHN BIGELOW,
Late Minister to France.

NEW YORK, 21 Grammercy Park,
Dec. 21, 1894.

GENTLEMEN, — Important engagements incident to the closing hours of the year will deprive me of the pleasure of joining personally in the well-merited tribute which it is proposed to pay to the biographer of Sumner on the 29th inst. It has rarely happened to our country to be so faithfully and effectively served officially as, for a quarter of a century, at least, it was served by Charles Sumner. It has yet more rarely happened to American statesmen to be so fortunate in their biographers.

None of our senators, I venture to affirm, have done more than Sumner to establish and maintain the highest standards of parliamentary dignity and authority ; and I can think of nothing likely to contribute so much to the perpetuation, or, if you please, to the restoration of those standards, as the biography by which the names of Charles Sumner and Edward L. Pierce are indissolubly associated in our literature. To the promotion of this patriotic interest the proposed testimonial of their common friends and admirers will, I would fain believe, prove an important and seasonable reinforcement.

I am, gentlemen, with great respect,
    Your very obedient servant,
        JOHN BIGELOW.

Hon. GEORGE F. HOAR,
  AND OTHERS.

LETTER FROM EX-GOVERNOR JOHN D. LONG.

FIFTH AVENUE HOTEL, NEW YORK,
Dec. 27, 1894.

DEAR MR. ERNST, — I have delayed answering your circular letter with regard to the dinner to Mr. Edward L. Pierce on Saturday next, hoping that I could arrange to be there. But the chance now is that I shall be detained here.

I read Mr. Pierce's "Life of Sumner" only a year ago, and I am glad that public acknowledgment is to be made for such a loyal, comprehensive, and valuable contribution to American literature. The author and the subject are both entitled to the tribute that is to be paid to them.

I came to know Mr. Pierce best in the Legislature of 1876, when he was Chairman of the Judiciary Committee and rendered very great service in that capacity. I thought then, and have thought ever since, that I have met no man with better capacity, not only for practical legislation, but for the higher moral influences that should attend public service. It is a matter of regret that he should not have served in the national councils. Mr. Sumner could not have a more fitting biographer. My most cordial regards to him.

Very truly yours,

JOHN D. LONG.

GEORGE A. O. ERNST, ESQ.

LETTER FROM SENATOR WILLIAM E. CHANDLER.

CONCORD, N. H., Dec. 27, 1894.

MY DEAR MR. HOAR, — With great pleasure I joined in the testimonial in recognition of Mr. Pierce and in commemoration of Mr. Sumner which is to find expression in our dinner of Saturday, December 29th, at the Parker House, and which I regret to find myself unable to attend.

Since my boyhood I have known and admired Mr. Pierce. He has been the friend of my mother and her family, who were natives of Canton, Mass.; and my own relations with him have been always near and helpful. Now that his task as biographer of Mr. Sumner has been so wisely, judiciously, and faithfully performed, I esteem it one of the highest privileges of my friendship to join in congratulating, praising, and thanking him for the superiority of his work.

Special circumstances have led me to take a deep interest in the Antislavery efforts of one of the three pioneers of freedom in the United States Senate, — John P. Hale. It must not be forgotten, when remembering Mr. Hale, Mr. Chase, and Mr. Sumner, that Mr. Hale was the first to enter the Senate. After the State election in New Hampshire in March, 1846, Mr. Whittier wrote triumphantly of the Free Soil victory, concluding, " Let the first wave of that northern flood, as it dashes against the walls of the Capitol, bear thither for the first time an Antislavery senator."

On December 6, 1847, Mr. Hale took his seat in the Senate, which contained 32 Democrats and 21 Whigs. An attempt being made to class him as a Whig, he repelled the classification, was excused by a vote of 17 to 16 from serving on committees, and he remained the only Free Soil senator until joined by Salmon P. Chase, on December 3, 1849, and by Charles Sumner, on December 1, 1851.

Whatever mistakes these great men, or any one of them, made in their long careers, they were giants in the conflict, and stand worthy of everlasting admiration and commendation. There were many difficulties in the way of opposing slavery under the Constitution as it stood. The Garrisonian method was the simplest: Destroy slavery, and with it the Constitution, if necessary. I am inclined to think that the course of Hale and Chase and Sumner was the better way: to expose and oppose slavery in every way possible, while saving the Constitution.

Mr. Lincoln felt the dilemma. From the only speech I heard him make, — one in Phenix Hall, in Concord, — I remember distinctly his exposition of the difference between his own and the pro-slavery class of politicians. He said in substance: We do not know precisely what we can do against slavery; but we do condemn it as a crime against humanity, and we call upon all who agree with us, henceforth and forever, in conducting the government, to deal with slavery as being *wrong*, and no longer to deal with it as being *right*. That is the change of principle and method which the Republicans propose to make.

To this work Mr. Sumner gave the herculean efforts of his life. He brought to it high literary culture, great legal learning, unsurpassed logical powers, and a zeal and fervor which would have made him — which did almost make him — a martyr to his cause. It is a great blessing to us all, that we have lived in the era which destroyed American chattel slavery; and reverently and gratefully I contemplate the picture, which the friend we to-day honor has graphically presented, of one of the greatest of the many liberty-loving orators and statesmen whom Massachusetts has given to the Nation.

Very respectfully,

WILLIAM E. CHANDLER.

Hon. GEORGE F. HOAR.

LETTER FROM JAMES B. ANGELL,
PRESIDENT OF THE UNIVERSITY OF MICHIGAN.

UNIVERSITY OF MICHIGAN, ANN ARBOR,
Dec. 22, 1894.

GENTLEMEN, — I beg to express my hearty thanks to you for the invitation to the dinner to be given on the 29th inst. to my college mate and old friend, Hon. Edward L. Pierce.

It is a fitting recognition of the high service Mr. Pierce has rendered to the memory of the great statesman, Charles Sumner, and to the history of one of the most eventful periods in the life of our nation. I regret extremely that my engagements here must deprive me of the pleasure of attending the dinner.

Yours very truly,

JAMES B. ANGELL.

Hon. GEORGE F. HOAR,
Hon. WILLIAM CLAFLIN,
AND OTHERS, *Committe.*

LETTER FROM RT.-REV. F. D. HUNTINGTON.

SYRACUSE, Dec. 18, 1894.

DEAR SIR, — It would be a special pleasure to me to be at the complimentary tribute to be paid to the Hon. Edward L. Pierce on the 29th, but engagements here put it out of my power. I beg leave to offer my highest regards to Mr. Sumner's distinguished biographer, and to thank your Committee for the honor of the invitation.

Sincerely,

F. D. HUNTINGTON.

To the Hon. GEORGE F. HOAR.

LETTER FROM MR. FRANK B. SANBORN.

CONCORD, Mass., Dec. 24, 1894.

DEAR MR. CLAFLIN, — I regret that a previous engagement, formed before I heard of the proposed dinner in honor of our friend, Mr. E. L. Pierce, will prevent me from testifying my regard for him, and my appreciation of his noble contribution to American political history, the "Life of Charles Sumner," by attending your festivity next Saturday.

It is very appropriate to call attention at this time to the public services of Senator Sumner, and the friends who upheld him in his long contest with the tyrannical, the selfish, the narrow-minded, and the timid, — yes, and with some good men, too, not so clear-sighted and observant as himself, — to maintain the inalienable rights of man on this new continent. It is all the more timely because a generation is growing up to whom the nature of that contest seems to be unfamiliar, and to whom various rhetoricians are addressing themselves, with the apparent intention, whether consciously or not, of concealing under smooth phrases and false generalizations the real issue in the warfare against negro slavery, which was met by the slave-masters with open war against the republic of Washington and Jefferson.

I noticed, a few days since, in the report of a copious and elaborate address given by one of these rhetoricians in Boston, — and, oddly enough, in the hall built as a memorial to Theodore Parker, grandson of the militia captain who did his duty at the opening of a Revolution in Lexington and Concord, — a phrase like this: " Revolutions never do good." As a startling paradox, an orator addressing a sleepy congregation might perhaps find it needful to say this; but to advance it seriously, as a proposition for history to support, and amid Christians, whose religion was and is a perpetual revolution, and in Boston, the city of two revolutions, both beneficent, seems to imply a loss of memory on the part of his hearers, and a stalwart sophistry in the orator himself, which will amaze or amuse, as we may look at it.

I take it neither Charles Sumner nor his biographer, nor those who will gather at your board to-day, had any aversion to the revolution in which the oligarchy of slave-masters, and their mercantile and office-holding tributaries in the Free States, was finally overthrown by the aroused moral sense and patriotism of the nation. That it should have to be done in the convulsion and amidst the perils of civil war was not the fault of our friends, but of those few myriads of interested and passionate men who had been cherishing what Brougham called "the wild and guilty fantasy that man can hold property in man." In the stress of that convulsion, and before those perils, neither Mr. Sumner nor Mr. Pierce hesitated to declare our national duty to an enslaved race; and they were among the first, as I remember, to pronounce for emancipation and for its natural sequel, — the enlistment and arming of the freedmen to defend the nation that had given them liberty, in the name of Jefferson's grand Declaration, and by the war-powers of Washington's wise Federal Constitution. It is for courage and foresight of this sort that statesmen are remembered: any two politicians can bargain and compromise, but it is only statesmen like Sumner who can settle the consequences of a revolution; and "nothing is ever settled that is not settled right," as Sumner said.

Yours faithfully,
F. B. SANBORN.

Hon. WILLIAM CLAFLIN, Boston.

LETTER FROM PROF. JAMES B. THAYER.

CAMBRIDGE, Dec. 28, 1894.

GENTLEMEN, — I had confidently expected to attend the dinner to-morrow in honor of Mr. Pierce and in commemoration of Mr. Sumner, the subject of his excellent biography; but an unexpected and imperative call requires my presence in a distant city.

As I cannot be present, I will ask leave to express now my sense of the great merits of Mr. Pierce's volumes, — the fruit of a devoted and self-forgetting friendship, of an extraordinary capacity for thorough research, of a wise and discriminating judgment, of sagacious reflection, of far-seeing patriotic sentiment.

Mr. Pierce and I have been old, almost lifelong, friends, and I shared to the full his early admiration of Mr. Sumner. For the young men of our generation whose moral sense had been aroused upon the subject of slavery, Sumner, far more than any other of our public men, was the great inspirer,

> "the chosen trump wherethrough
> Our God sent forth awakening breath."

In the long, stern fight that he maintained until slavery went down, he was always the idealist, the believer in the glory and dignity of human nature, who, through all disguises, conventions, and illusions, saw clearly the hideous, naked barbarity of slavery, and poured out upon it with an unmeasured utterance his execration, his loathing, and disgust. Others might listen to excuses, to palliations, to suggestions of delay or composition, — not he! From him there came and could come nothing but indignation and instant, unsparing denunciation for a thing so foul, so shameful, so dishonoring to God and man.

Mr. Pierce's book has many claims upon our admiration. One of the chief of them is that it preserves and fixes ineffaceably in our annals the aspect of Sumner to which I have referred, — the figure of a great, relentless moral hero, fighting the battle of human nature itself to its successful end.

Wishing you, gentlemen, and your honored guest, all possible enjoyment of to-morrow's occasion, and deeply regretting my own inability to share it, I am, with much respect,

Very truly yours,
JAMES B. THAYER.

Hon. WILLIAM CLAFLIN
  AND OTHERS, *Committee.*

LETTER FROM JUSTIN WINSOR OF HARVARD UNIVERSITY.

CAMBRIDGE, 74 Sparks Street, Dec. 18, 1894.

DEAR SIR, — I have, from the Committee, an invitation to unite in the dinner to be given to Mr. Pierce on Dec. 29th, and exceedingly regret my inability to become one of his testifying friends on such an occasion. I have duties in Washington that week, and shall not get home in season.

The book which is associated with Mr. Pierce's name is about the best American historic contemporary biography which I know, and he deserves a signal recognition.

Very truly yours,
JUSTIN WINSOR.

MR. GEORGE A. O. ERNST.

LETTER FROM MILTON M. FISHER,

AN ANTISLAVERY VETERAN.

MEDWAY, Dec. 28, 1894.

GENTLEMEN, — I am pleased to receive an invitation to a complimentary dinner to Hon. Edward L. Pierce, and also commemorative of Charles Sumner, to be given the 29th instant. At my advanced age (being nearly eighty-four), and with some infirmities, I might well be excused if absent; but I could not excuse myself without some word in commemoration of Mr. Sumner, and expressing the great joy his affiliation and influence gave, especially to that portion of the Antislavery party which recognized the ballot as an essential element in the overthrow of the slave-power.

On May 5th, 1834, the first public meeting of the American Antislavery Society was held in New York, with delegates from all the Free States. It was my privilege to be an accredited delegate from Massachusetts, and my good fortune now to be the only surviving delegate from this State or any other, — with possibly one exception, that of Robert Purvis, a colored gentleman from Philadelphia. The Liberty party, which I assisted in forming, cast seven thousand votes in 1840, and sixty thousand in 1844. The annexation of Texas, and other events, hastened a crisis; and the public utterances of men prominent in affairs of state were carefully scanned during the next four years. Among the brilliant men of that period in the Whig party, Charles Sumner appeared to be coming into sympathy with the new party. His oration of July 4, 1845; his speech Nov. 4, 1845, against the admission of Texas as a Slave State; and later, his address against the abduction of an escaped slave, — gave hope of a closer connection with it.

In the spring of 1848, Hon. Warren Lovering, a prominent member of the Whig party, and myself, wishing to learn the currents of public opinion, sought interviews one day with Henry Wilson, whom we did not find at home, and with Mr. Sumner, whom we succeeded in finding at his law-office in Boston, where I was introduced to him by my friend as an old Abolitionist and Liberty-party man. In the course of the conversation I asked Mr. Sumner if he knew Salmon P. Chase, and he answered, "Yes, and I am now in correspondence with him upon the present crisis." I then asked, "Are you in harmony with his views?" and he replied, "I am." I cannot recall any other moment of my political life which gave me such a thrill of joy and hope as when these words came from his own lips; and I may safely say that when known, no declaration of any man in the State ever gave the old Abolitionists such intense satisfaction as his open affiliation with their aggressive movement against the slave system, which began seventeen years before. From this time until the day of his death, he was one of our political idols. I speak from the standpoint of the earliest Abolitionists, who believed in united political action on the slavery question. In all subsequent interviews with this man of the highest culture, whether upon the street in the city or in the Senate at Washington, he was no less courteous and cordial in his personal relations than devoted to the cause to which he had committed himself in the spirit of a martyr — as in fact he was.

It was at least fortunate, if not specially provided by his sagacity and personal friendship, that the history of his life-work, and of the times in which he lived, was intrusted to one so sympathetic with him in his spirit and career, and so competent to give to the world such a picture as our honored guest has successfully given of a true patriot and statesman, deserving honor and renown among the noblest and best in all lands.

Respectfully yours,

MILTON M. FISHER.

To Hon. WILLIAM CLAFLIN,
AND OTHERS.

LETTER FROM REV. JOHN W. CHADWICK.

626 CARLTON AVE., BROOKLYN, N. Y.,
Dec. 27, 1894.

DEAR SIRS, — It would give me great pleasure to unite with your Committee and the friends whom you invite, in doing honor to Mr. Pierce for his great accomplishment, but the press of my engagements renders it impossible for me to indulge my inclination. I shall await with interest but without anxiety a report of what is said at the dinner. I am confident that Mr. Pierce's "Life of Sumner" will be nobly praised; and also that it cannot be praised in excess of its deserts. It is more than a great biography of a great man. It is a great history of a great time, all of which Sumner saw, and a great part of which he was; and that Mr. Pierce has not exaggerated that part, but rightly estimated its proportion to the parts taken by others, is one of the most marked and interesting features of his work. It is to me a marvel of fidelity, of patience, of lucidity, of fairness to all concerned. I remember with pleasure the satisfaction Mr. Pierce expressed with my review of the concluding volumes in the New York "Nation" and "Evening Post;" but I knew well enough that his satisfaction was much more an indication of his modesty than of my success. I now think of that review as miserably inadequate. It did not begin to express my sense of the distinguished intellectual and moral qualities of Mr. Pierce's biography of the great statesman whom he was privileged to call his friend and made his title clear.

I shall miss not only the praises due to Mr. Pierce, but also those which the memory of Sumner will evoke. These I am sure will be more grateful to Mr. Pierce than those which he himself receives, for they will in some measure assure him that the one great object of his busy life is sure of its attainment, and that the name and fame of Sumner will enjoy that great distinction in the State of Massachusetts and throughout our whole nation which is their just due.

Gentlemen of the Committee, I am, with warmest sympathy for the enterprise in which you are engaged,

Yours very respectfully,

JOHN WHITE CHADWICK.

Messrs. WILLIAM CLAFLIN
AND OTHERS, *Committee.*

LETTER FROM REV. JAMES O. MURRAY.

DEAN'S OFFICE, COLLEGE OF NEW JERSEY,
PRINCETON, Dec. 23, 1894.

MY DEAR SIR, — I beg to acknowledge with many thanks the invitation to the dinner in honor of the Hon. Edward L. Pierce, on the completion of his biography of Charles Sumner. It brought before my mind days long past when Mr. Pierce and myself were fellow-students in Brown University. The friendship then formed has endured through all the intervening years. I have rejoiced in all the honors he has enjoyed, and most of all perhaps in that which is now proposed, the recognition of his admirable success as the biographer of Sumner.

Unless my memory deceives me, when he entered college in 1846 he was a tolerably fierce Democrat, as parties then stood. But before he was graduated, under the influence of Dr. Wayland and Mr. Sumner, it was evident that in the coming struggle between freedom and slavery he would be found among the stanchest and boldest opponents of slavery. It has been pleasant also for me to recall the fact, that in his college days he showed the aptitudes and pursued the studies inside and outside the college curriculum which have made him so accomplished a biographer. Again thanking you for the invitation of the Committee, and regretting my inability to be present at the dinner, I am, with great respect,

Yours truly,

JAMES O. MURRAY.

To Hon. GEORGE F. HOAR.

Among the gentlemen who sent letters sympathetic with the occasion and expressing regret at their inability to be present were: Rev. Samuel May, of Leicester; Rev. A. P. Putnam, of Concord; William H. Baldwin, of Boston; Francis A. Walker, President Massachusetts Institute of Technology; George H. Monroe, of Brookline; Merrill E. Gates, President of Amherst College; Hiram Barney, of New York; Rev. James G. Vose, of Providence, R. I.; Moses Pierce, of Norwich, Conn.; and Orville H. Platt, U. S. Senator from Connecticut.

www.ingramcontent.com/pod-product-compliance
Lightning Source LLC
Chambersburg PA
CBHW020324090426
42735CB00009B/1388